elmar
hahn
verlag

Mainfranken

A Pictorial Journey through Main-Franconia

Impressum:

© Elmar Hahn Verlag,
Raiffeisenstr. 2, 97209 Veitshöchheim, Germany
www.elmar-hahn-verlag.de

Idea and Concept: Elmar Hahn, Klaus Schinagl

Text: Thomas Huth, Frankfurt

English interpretation: Dr. Terence Zuber,
    New Martinsville, WV

Photography: Elmar Hahn

except

Rudolf Diemer – pages: 16, 17 left below

Cornelia Haas – page 58 right

Gerhard Hagen – page: 31 left

Jürgen Holzhausen – pages: 18, 19 right, 20, 34/35

Thomas Huth – page: 8

Anton Kaiser – pages: 15, 17 right, 19 left above,
23 right, 24/25, 27, 29, 32, 39 right

Herbert Liedel – pages: 2/3, 144

Arnulf Müller – page: 21

Wolfgang Pusch – pages: 12/13

Claus Schenk – page: 14

Staatliche Kurverwaltung Bad Kissingen – page: 30

Stephan Thierfelder – page: 37

Layout: Design by Klaus Schinagl,
    Veitshöchheim – www.schinagl.de

Production: Druckerei Theiss GmbH,
    St. Stefan im Lavanttal – www.theiss.at

ISBN 978-3-928645-52-2

Main-Franconia – a Harmonious Orchestration 6

The Land of Far Horizons The Franconian Rhön Hills 13

Woods, Wine and Red Rock
The Meandering Main River Divides the Spessart Hills and the Odenwald Forest 35

A Triangle Full of Grapes A Geometric Design on the Main 67

History Characterizes the Present Würzburg – Main-Franconia's Cultural Center 95

Knights Ruled the Hills The Steigerwald Wood and the Hassberg Hills 131

Main-Franconia – a Harmonious Orchestration

For a stretch of countryside that does not actually exist, at least one that cannot be found on a map of Germany, Main-Franconia is very much a region worth enjoying! In order to locate this region, start by looking for Lower Franconia, named such by the Bavarian government. It encompasses the area between the Spessart Hills and the Steigerwald Wood in addition to the Rhön Hills south to the Tauber River. Another reason for the name Main-Franconia is due to the presence of the Main River, but once again, Main-Franconia in itself is not a geographic unit. The connection here is of a cultural and scenic nature and has little to do with administrative borders that divide all of Franconia into three distinct regions: Upper, Middle and Lower Franconia. There was never a state named Franconia on the banks of the Main River. There were, nonetheless, self-governing city-republics and secular duchies not to mention the prince-bishops of Würzburg whose religious power and influence dwarfed everything else. From a Franconian point of view, the prince-bishop represented a major power and it is a fact that the prince-bishop wielded a great amount of influence culturally. His role was one of a con-

ductor directing the various provincial rulers in harmonious orchestration. Leaving the Roman settlements along the Main River out of consideration, more recent history in Main-Franconia begins with the bishopric in Würzburg. St. Burkard, Würzburg's first bishop (741/742) began the long line that continues to the present. In the year 689, three Irish missionaries, Kilian, Kolonat and Todnan died as martyrs in Würzburg. Not long after they were found decapitated, Würzburg's sole secular ruling family, the Thuringian-Frankish dynasty, died out. The power vacuum was soon filled by the founding of the bishopric and this political and cultural force lasted until the end of the Holy Roman Empire of the German Nation in 1803. It is most likely due to this unusually long period of continuity that no other city in Lower Franconia could even come close in importance and influence to Würzburg. In a manner of speaking, Würzburg was to Main-Franconia what Rome was to Italy: it dominated without really ruling. The main reason for this was the fact that the Main-Franconian countryside varied too greatly and

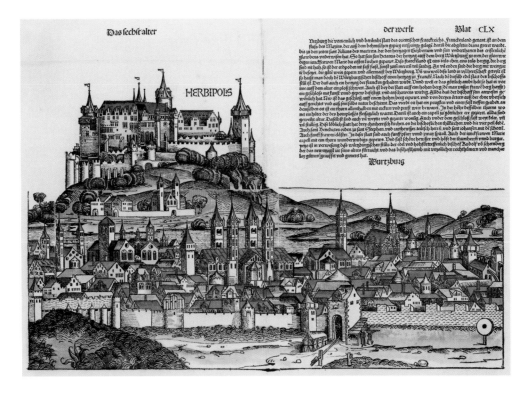

Würzburg in Schedel's World Chronicle in 1492

6

Main-Franconia was considered more or less to be transit country. There were and are no real topographic borders; even the Rhön Hills, the highest just over 900 meters, don't form a natural border. Instead, they serve as a link between north and south Germany. This link serves as a cultural transition and not as an abrupt rupture. Main-Franconia has always been a region open to and curious about its neighbors' innovations. Whether it was architectural styles or fashion, religious or secular movements such as the Reformation or the Peasants' War, Main-Franconia was never the birthplace of any revolutionary ideas or movements. Nevertheless, it did concern itself with the world beyond its borders, fervently discussed current events, and took a decision on the goings-on. The strategic location of Main-Franconia in the heart of Germany made it highly advisable to make the best out of the situation at hand. An excellent example is the churches: fine specimens of every architectural style from Romanesque to modern dot the countryside. Such a representative collection can hardly be found elsewhere in all of the country. Moreover, Catholics and Protestants alike lived side by side. The jubilance of excess was celebrated in the Rococo church in Amorbach, a former Benedictine monastery and located just a few kilometers away from the former counts of Wertheim who took Calvinism deadly serious.

Life was, by no means, always peaceful. Diversity led to serious confrontations and in the Middle Ages, even to regional wars. Over the centuries, people did stick together and differences were ironed out time and again. Such close proximity taught Main-Franconians to see that their differences were not that great and that sometimes differences nurtured healthy competition. This is

best illustrated by taking a short drive from Würzburg along the Main River to Kitzingen. Almost each and every fortified hamlet along the route had its own ruler: the prince-bishop of Würzburg, a canon, the Count von Limpurg, the margraves of Ansbach, the von Schwarzenberg princes or the Zobel family in Giebelstadt. Every one of these rulers walled in his valuable possessions, participated in commercial trade on the river, improved on the infrastructure by building harbors, bridges and roads, and sponsored the construction of representative stately buildings such as the picture perfect Town Hall in Sulzfeld or the parish church in Sommerhausen. Competition was keen, the river was crucial to trade and wine ensured prosperity. Competition and the economy flourished from the 15th century to the Thirty Years' War (1618-1648). Proof of this fact can be seen between Ochsenfurt and Volkach: there is one ornate town hall after another, each truly a jewel in its own right. Nowhere else in Germany can the traveler find such a density of fortified towns that so obviously display the self-confidence of the landed gentry. Volkach's Town Hall which features a freestanding outer staircase, arches and oriels and spacious council chambers manifests this confidence. Protecting one's possessions, whether of material nature or age-old privileges and freedoms, meant erecting a wall. Market towns were just as fortified as cities holding a city charter. The more watchtowers, the more threatening the village looked from afar. The number of gates a town could afford might also make a town look "better" than its neighbor. A prime example is Dettelbach, which was

▲ *The minnesinger, Walther von der Vogelweide, is laid to rest in Würzburg*

granted a city charter in 1484, and in celebration of this freedom had over 50 towers erected. It was a magnificent sight to behold. The fact that the towers were militarily insignificant and would never have offered any real protection was of no concern. The city opened its coffers and built a so-called decorative wall of celebration.

The southern portion of the Main River Triangle and the western part of the foothills to the Steigerwald Wood were extremely well-heeled and such follies could be easily financed. This was not the case in other parts of Main-Franconia. There, it was not a matter of displaying wealth; it was mainly a matter of making a living. The fertile, densely-populated countryside surrounding Schweinfurt and Würzburg stood in stark contrast to the higher plateaus of the sparsely-populated Rhön Hills and the interior of the Spessart Hills where there was little more than a thicket of trees. In fact, travelers normally circumvented the Spessart and when no other route was possible, passed through as quickly as possible. For this reason, the oldest settlements and the few towns are located along the edge of the hills in the Main and Kinzig valleys. It wasn't until the 18th century

that attempts were made to establish a glass and an iron industry, both of which were short lived. Farming on poor soil was not an option. Those who settled in towns like Rechtenbach, Weibersbrunn or Heinrichsthal evidently had nothing to lose by leaving their former homesteads. More often than not, a settler had to be satisfied with a narrow strip of land between the forest and his humble abode at the side of the road. This multipurpose strip of land was used to raise one's daily fare, keep goats and supply wood for the fire. It was a simple existence in this never-ending line of roadside settlements whose names often ended in –thal or valley. It wasn't until after World War II that life changed radically for the better and economic prosperity finally reached the region. It was the autobahn that made it possible to commute to industrial centers to work. Although the villages changed as well, many of the simple structures retained their outer facades including their typical "yodeling" balconies. Despite the favorable changes, the region remained loyal to the Rhine-Main region, because for centuries, large portions

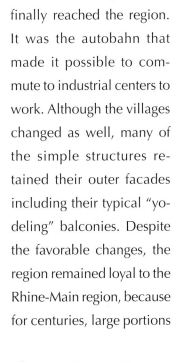

A Schönborn family gathering as depicted on the High Altar in Gaibach

of the Spessart Hills had belonged to the archbishop of Mainz and Lower Franconia was called "Lower Franconia and Aschaffenburg."

The Rhön Hills to the north are a similar case. Kreuzberg Hill and the hills of the High Rhön are a world of their own. The heart of Main-Franconia has little in common with the Rhön Hills where the climate is harsh, the topographic preconditions poor, and the infrastructure deficient. At least the Spessart Hills has a navigable river along its border; something the high hills of the Rhön do not. Emigration from the Rhön Hills was the normal course of events and only along the Streu and Brend streams were living conditions somewhat more favorable. Old urban centers such as Fladungen, Bischofsheim and Ostheim stand out in an otherwise unpopulated area. Nowadays, the contrast between the isolated high plateaus featuring rounded hilltops and moorland and the more densely-populated valleys opens doors for tourism in the Rhön. It has become a natural reserve and conservationists are doing their utmost to preserve the flora and fauna and general natural beauty of these hills.

The region to the east of the heart of Main-Franconia, the Hassberg Hills and Steigerwald Wood, pose less of a contrast. Gently rolling hills, none higher than 500 meters, characterize an area that for hundreds of years was divided among several families of the landed gentry. It is interesting to seek out these peculiarities that are still evident today, be it in the fertile farmlands or in the cities and towns. Nowhere else in Germany did nobility assert itself so persistently as in the Hassberg Hills. The Lichtenstein, Rotenhan, Sternberg, Bibra and Truchsess families, to name just a few, had an entire string of castles built atop the rolling hills between Bad Königshofen and Sesslach. These were very clear symbols of power in this rural countryside and the rulers' subjects were not that poorly off because these rulers, for better or worse, depended heavily on their subjects' subservience. In fact, these peasants were better off than in other parts of Main-Franconia; village breweries and bakeries as well as communal halls were built for their convenience and enjoyment. The Knights' Chapel in Hassfurt displays the family coats-of arms, a type of who's who for Franconian nobility, in its elegant late Gothic Ritterkapelle. The Hassberg Hills and the Steigerwald Wood were an agreeable mixture of agrarian life and lesser nobility. Nowadays, farming no longer provides a viable income and commuting has become a way of life for those living in these laid-back regions. Most commute to Schweinfurt to work in the world-famous ball bearing factories. During the 19th and 20th centuries, this former free imperial city grew in importance and became the region's number one industrial site. It wasn't only a few major inventions that created an

▲ *A romantic view of Miltenberg in the 19th century*

9

economic wonder; it was the potential workforce that was no longer subject to and dependent on the aristocracy outside the city as well as swiftly increasing birthrates that enabled the smooth transition from free imperial city to a modern industrial city. A Renaissance Town Hall and production plants are both at home in Schweinfurt.

It would be doing the city an injustice if the fact that Schweinfurt is known for its wine were not mentioned. Silvaner, Müller-Thurgau, Bacchus and several other typically Franconian varieties flourish on the Petersstirn slopes. From here, it is a stone's throw to the Franconian vineyards in the heart of Main-Franconia: the Main River Triangle. A rich cultural heritage and winegrowing characterize this unique region where the arts and viticulture link the past to the future. Traditions remain strong and they have laid the groundwork for a prosperous tomorrow. The best place to experience the culmination of tradition and cultural heritage is Würzburg, a spiritually-influenced city where churches, convents and monasteries, and Crusading orders have left their mark. Everything from the numerous madonnas on the building facades and in the niches to the grand procession of saints on the Old Main Bridge remind the traveler of the role that religion has played. The city's architecture alone makes a visit worthwhile. Würzburg boasts a Romanesque Cathedral whose construction as seen today was begun in 1040; a Gothic church dedicated to the Virgin at the Market Place, the site of the former Jewish ghetto; a sumptuous Baroque Residence built by the prince-bishops whose religious and secular power dominated until 1803; a Rococo inn, the House to the Falcon, that now houses the library and a Rococo chapel, the Court Chapel, that served as the prince-bishops' private chapel in the Residence. Needless to say, church towers abound and the best view of these spires as well as the city itself is from Marienberg Fortress perched on the hill above the Main River. By the time the arches of the first stone bridge across the Main were completed in 1133, the bishop had already acquired the most important sovereign rights for the town. As a safety precaution, in 1253 he transferred his residence in the town to the recently fortified Marienberg Fortress, the stronghold of the bishops against the townspeople for centuries to follow.

The view from the fortress also includes the surrounding countryside and the sun soaked vineyard slopes. Franconian wines grow on various types of soil throughout the Main River Triangle and in the Steigerwald Wood: shell limestone, variegated sandstone, bedrock, clay and keuper are some of the more common types of soil that in combination with the climate have such distinct effects on the bouquet and the taste of the wine. The noblest appellations are Stein wines grown on the slopes of the Main River. As early as the 16th century, the saying "the best wine grows on the Stein" was an indication of

◀ *Schweinfurt before industrialization*

its quality. Würzburg's charitable institutions, the Juliusspital and the Bürgerspital, produce Absleite, Pfaffenberg and Kirchberg appellations. The state-run Hofkellerei or Court Cellars in the Residence is the third large winery in Würzburg. The Bocksbeutel or flat-bellied wine bottle is typical to Main-Franconia and conscientious vintners only bottle their premium wines in such bottles. Numerous wine pubs and inns throughout the city provide the traveler the opportunity to relax and savor a "Schoppen" (¼ liter) of Franconian wine, an authentic part of the Würzburg's heritage.

Among the most significant works of art are the masterpieces of two Franconian craftsmen: the sculptor, Tilman Riemenschneider, and the architect, Balthasar Neumann. Their works embody the tastes and the character of Main-Franconians and their influence has left an impressively distinctive mark on the entire region. Riemenschneider, known as the "gentle tyrant," had little success with his woodcarvings outside Franconia. On the other hand, he was so popular in and around Würzburg that no other craftsman had a chance. His works speak for an entire epoch. Riemenschneider without Main-Franconia is just as unlikely as Main-Franconia without Riemenschneider. More than 200 years later, Balthasar Neumann came to the region and combined his great technical versatility with his appreciation for aesthetic splendor in everything from a simple keyhole to water pipes, from row houses and churches to the Residence in Würzburg. His intuitive feeling for proportions enabled him to create his own Main-Franconian version of the Baroque and his work is renowned far outside the borders of Germany. Neumann was capable of linking his adopted homeland to the outside world, of turning local characteristics into international trends. Main-Franconia has the ingredients for a successful future. Enjoy!

▶ *William Harriot's painting of the Cathedral in Würzburg in the 19th century*

The Land
of Far Horizons

The Franconian Rhön Hills

If you have never been to the Rhön Hills, you might nonetheless gather from the rough sound of the word itself that this is a rugged region. And for a fact, these hills in the heart of Germany are known for their rather harsh beauty and somewhat bracing climate. Whether or not the word Rhön was actually chosen to describe this region may never be known since the origin of the word is prior to written records and not Germanic. Another problem was defining the boundaries of the Rhön Hills. For hundreds of years, only the central High Rhön region was considered the Rhön while the entire area between the Sinn and Werra rivers was known as

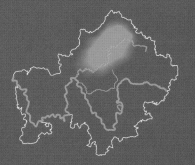

◀ *The black-faced Rhön sheep graze on the hillsides*

"Buchonia." It is also interesting to note that the town of Bischofsheim added "near the Rhön" to its official name while Ostheim described itself as "at the foothills of the Rhön." Nowadays, both of these towns are considered to be in the heart of the Rhön Hills. At the time these names were conferred on these towns, no one ever thought of linking this name with a pristine, unspoiled countryside ideal for leisure time activities. Actually, quite the opposite was the case for years on end. The Rhön Hills conjured up the impression of dire circumstances and a humble, hard life. It should be no surprise then that Bischofsheim found it important to attach "near the Rhön" to its name so that there would be no mistaking the town's location: it was not "in" the Rhön Hills. It is a fact that for decades the people who inhabited these volcanic hills and farmed the high, infertile hilltops were poverty-stricken. Yields barely fed the families themselves and making ends meet meant taking on odd jobs such as making wooden shoes, performing as an amateur musician or weaving on a loom in the already overcrowded main room of the family dwelling. People emigrated time and again and many a town was left deserted. As late as the 19th century, the saying still went: "The Rhön provides the most soldiers, parsons and prostitutes" in Franconia and those who stayed behind consoled themselves with hard liquor. In 1826, Karl Julius Weber commented laconically, "It is a shame that so many have fallen victim to spirits." Fortunately, these good old days are a thing of the past. The Open Air Museum in Fladungen offers an informative walk into a destitute, down-and-out way of life in the Rhön Hills. An everyday lifestyle that might seem quaint and idyllic nowadays was anything but romantic for the hard-working farmers of these hills. The impression the traveler has when he leaves these rounded hilltops for the spa town of Bad Kissingen is quite a different one. An elegant world of luxury and grandeur appears more like a mirage than reality. Praise for the healing effects of the waters from diverse springs in the Rhön Hills had been sung for generations, but it wasn't until the 19th century that industrialization and train travel made it possible to take advantage of such medicinal waters. For the first time, the well-heeled and the mighty, nobility and statesmen as well as patrician burghers had both the time and money to spend several weeks in such surroundings. Bad Kissingen was blessed with healing waters as well as the ruling Wittelsbach dynasty and it became one of Germany's most popular spa resorts prior to World War I. The spa town of Bad Brückenau could have participated in this boom as well but its location on the Sinn River was a disadvantage: the town lay too deep in the hills to provide these spa guests with the necessary glamour they desired. The wide valley of the Franconian Saale River, on the other hand, was ideal for the construction of stately, posh edifices that were representative of the guests who resided there. Nowadays the guests are on a tighter

◀ *Winter in the Rhön Hills creates a stark contrast between the black basalt rock and the white snow*

budget and wellness programs and golf courses are the current trend but the Prince Regent architectural style still dominates Bad Kissingen and remains reminiscent of an era when Europe's monarchs drank from the potent wells and enjoyed a rendezvous or two. Three Bavarian kings, Ludwig I through III; Bismarck; Emperor Franz Josef and his beautiful wife, Sissi; Russian Czar Alexander II as well as numerous illustrious members of nobility laid the groundwork for our present day desire for free time activites and holiday-making. The average holiday-maker nowadays, however, is more likely to want to travel to more exotic parts of the world than to take the waters in a Franconian spa and is probably more interested in having fun than rejuvenation massages. In an ever-expanding world of globalization, the Rhön Hills with its mineral waters has to alter its strategy to encourage a new order of clientele. One of the alternatives at hand involves biosphere reserves in vast portions of the region. The Rhön spreads over the states of Bavaria, Thuringia and Hesse and cooperation among these states is helping to take advantage of a formidable opportunity to improve the environment as well the economic structure of the region. The Rhön has no industry or services sector to grow the economy; it is sparsely populated by German standards: only 65 inhabitants per square kilometer. Moreover, the infrastructure cannot begin to compete with metropolitan areas. Its greatest resources are the natural beauty of a pristine countryside and the proximity to cultural events. One of the region's mottos is: "Products from the region for the region." This may be the only feasible way to preserve the character of this austere hilly region without forcing its inhabitants to leave. One success story involves the long-legged, black-faced sheep pastured on the hills that add a bucolic touch to the scenery as well as variety to local menus. Lamb roast, lamb sausage and salami as well as fresh lamb's cheese have become regional culinary specialties. Orchards of fallen fruit that contribute to the idyllic transition between inhabited villages and open countryside are also growing in importance. The region is undergoing an exciting transformation from fruit brandy distilleries to an exemplary ecological biotope.

▲ *Misty winter days allow for spectacular lighting*

A Lesson in Geology – the Rhön's Volcanic Past

There is evidence of former volcanic activity almost everywhere in the Rhön Hills. Volcanic eruptions 18 to 25 million years ago caused streams of lava to flow and solidify to form the basalt boulders that are so predominant nowadays. There are over 500 basalt chimneys: everything from slopes of scree to a weather-worn basalt layer on Schafstein Hill ◄ to the sharp-edged basalt prisms on Gangolfsberg Hill ▲. At one time, basalt was mined and used to cobblestone streets, reinforce quays and provide ballast for train tracks throughout Germany. Unspoiled countryside can still be found in the Thuringian part of the Rhön Hills ▶.

The Rhön Hills present a landscape of contrasts. One moment the hiker is admiring the basalt boulders that resulted from lava solidifying in layers and a few steps further, the ground turns into boggy marshland. Islands of vegetation ◀ feign firm ground but then the eye discovers the bog holes, the so-called eyes of the moor ▶, and nothing seems as it is. Fortunately, an elevated wooden path enables the hiker to walk through the Black Moor and become acquainted with its rare wildflowers such as the insectivorous sundew plant and numerous species of rushes as well as the Carpathian birch tree ▼.

Along a Wooden Path to Bog Holes and Sundew

The Black Moor ◄► and its panoramic views are the great attraction of the so-called Long Rhön. Unlike other moors in this region, the spa resorts never cut the peat here and as a result, over the last several thousand years, six to seven meters of peat layers have been forming in a water impermeable basin. Thanks to 1000 millimeters of precipitation, 150 days of frost and approximately 200 days of fog per annum, peat continues to form though ever so slowly at about a millimeter a year. The success of the 60-hectare large Black Moor is due in part to the fact that it has served as a nature reserve since 1939 and mankind has not interfered. The second largest high moor, the Red Moor, on the other hand, is an example of how lengthy and arduous the process of returning a moor to its original state is. Peat cutting left half of the area depleted and centuries will pass before the scars of such cuttings are healed. Reforestation in the 20th century also changed the appearance of the High Rhön previously known for its wide open scenery.

A Thousand-Year Old Creation Depleted in a Few Decades

Rural Life Abounds in the Hamlets

Although Ostheim at the foothills of the Rhön has had a city charter since the 16th century, for generations on end, its townspeople were mainly tillers of the soil. In order to protect their possessions in times of war, they built a stately fortified church ▲ similar to their neighbors in Nordheim ◄. Just how simple and unromantic rural life once was can be experienced in the Open Air Museum in Fladungen ◄ ◄. No matter how lovely the High Rhön was and still is, those who eked a living on remote farmsteads ▲ had little leisure time to ponder the natural beauty of the region.

Nobility preferred the foothills of the Rhön where the fertile soil produced higher yields to the harsh, windswept ridges at higher altitudes. The moated castle in Unsleben ◀, noted for its varying architectural styles incorporated over the centuries, is one of the jewels in the wide Streu valley. Several noble families owned and resided in Salzburg Fortress ▶ above Bad Neustadt. Mary Magdalene Church in Münnerstadt contains Tilman Riemenschneider's first carved altar ▼.

Knights' Residences and a Riemenschneider Altar

Aschach – A Treasure Trove along the Franconian Saale

The locals talk about the fortresses along "Saale Beach." They are referring to the Saxony Saale River, the big sister of the Franconian Saale. The fact that the Franconian Saale meanders ▲ from its source in Grabfeld to the mouth of the Main after 135 kilometers passing innumerable stately homes and castles is less well known. Aschach Castle and its outbuildings ◀ are a prime example of how a number of noble families like the counts of Henneberg, bishops, and Wilhelm Sattler, a 19th century industrialist, lent a hand to the creation of this gem.

When Germans were surveyed a few years back as to which resort came to mind when the word "Bad" or spa was mentioned, most of them mentioned Bad Kissingen located on the Franconian Saale. In the years prior to the First World War, the movers and shakers and beautiful people gathered in this peaceful summer resort town to take the healing waters. The list of celebrities included everyone from the Russian czar and his family to Austrian Empress Elisabeth, German kings and princes and political giants such as Chancellor Bismarck and the German artist, Adolph von Menzel. The Prince-Regent Concert Hall ◀, the Arcades ▼ and inviting spa courtyard ▶ are reminiscent of the elegant epoch of Prince-Regent Luipold.

Where the Rich and the Mighty Took the Waters

Where the Saale River Once Flowed Past Prince-Bishops

The town of Hammelburg was situated in the southernmost corner of Main-Franconia, which first belonged to the prince-abbot and later to the prince-bishop of Fulda. In 777 Charlemagne had bestowed the Franconian fort on the new monastery and it was in this document that winegrowing in Franconia was officially mentioned. The prince-bishops of Fulda resided in and left their mark on this town on the Saale ◄. Their impressive Baroque "administrative castle" ► was built by the court architect, Andrea Gallasini. Fortress Trimburg ▲ dominates an outcrop on the hilltop a few kilometers further up the river. At one time, there were three Trimburg fortresses here; unfortunately, only parts of the middle fortress have survived.

Woods, Wine and Red Rock

The Meandering Main River Divides the Spessart Hills and the Odenwald Forest

Driving on the A3 highway, the traveler can cross through the Spessart Hills between Aschaffenburg and Wertheim in a good half hour. The drive is scenic providing a glimpse of a variety of deciduous trees and deeply-carved valleys with few settlements in sight. The sparsely-populated Spessart Hills is one of the largest continuous forested areas in Germany. For this very reason, the area was bypassed for hundreds of years. A trip through these hills 200 years ago was

◀ Beech and oak trees stand proudly in the Spessart Hills

truly an adventure. The roads were indistinguishable and bands of robbers seemed to lurk at every bend. No one was ever sure when or where the Spessart robbers would attack or what their price would be: money, life and limb or both? The distance between the halfway risk-free hamlets was great and the remote inns along the way were seldom safe havens. Passing through these woods wasn't any more dangerous than through other similar hilly regions in Germany but in 1828 Wilhelm Hauff immortalized tales of murder and theft in his book *The Pub in the Spessart*.

This book became popular because, at the time, people wanted entertaining spine-chilling adventures in order to feel safe in their everyday lives. However, many a hair-raising ballad was sung about the sinister doings of

▲ *Fortified elegance: Henneburg Fortress above Stadtprozelten*

these robbers, which did little to abate the traveler's imagination:

"The traveler's flesh creeps and he is terrified
By the thought of going through the wood,
Where evil robbers dwell and where the devil's blunderbuss bangs,
Each and every life is threatened!
Some are already dead as a doornail!
Traveler, be cautious
Since the robbers keep watch in the dark wood."

The truth of the matter was that these woodsmen were more or less forced to do some robbing on the side because the forests were rarely owned by the people who inhabited them. Knotted oaks and game abounded but in great part, they belonged to the archbishop of Mainz who had received the forests in appreciation for his services to the Emperor and the Empire in the 11th century. The question these robbers asked themselves went something like: why not take something from the wealthier that are evidently living comfortably and divide some of that wealth among the needy, among ourselves? The robbed who "contributed" to this welfare scheme at least had the opportunity to see who was benefiting from their generosity. However, none of these involuntary contributors were the slightest bit interested in either parting with their fortune or becoming acquainted with their benefactors. Draconian punishments were imposed and carried out. Hangings were common and provided a form of entertainment among decent folk and those not yet caught. Even today the mention of the word "Spessart" reminds the average German of rustling leaves and pistol shots accompanied by screams of horror emerging from a deep, dark forest.

The Spessart Museum in Lohr manages to dispel this cliché effectively in its informative documentation of the 19th century.

The word Spessart translates into "Woodpecker Wood" in English and although the Spessart is centrally located in Germany, it has remained thinly-populated. History and geology have played a major role. The largest portion of the Spessart is red sandstone, an aesthetic building material with its warm red hues made manifest in the Aschaffenburg Castle. However, as subsoil for growing crops, it can hardly be considered fertile. Previous generations who lived off their fields found no reason to settle in the region. Stone quarries here and in several areas bordering on the Spessart that had easy access to transport on the Main River could eke out a decent living but there was never any real money in red sandstone. Natural resources weren't really an option either since there were too few for any long-term investments. There was some copper, zinc, lead and silver to be mined near Bieber and there were the minerals mined to make pencils near the town of Klingenberg, but that is an entirely different story. The Spessart just didn't offer any viable means of making a living over a longer period of time. Even the glass industry near Lohr, financed by the electors of Mainz in the 18th century, was productive for only a few generations. In the same manner, iron

 *Mist covers the woods*

manufacturing fell victim to cheaper production elsewhere. There wasn't much to attract anyone to settle in the region; life was simply too hard. To be truthful, there actually wasn't that much land available since large portions of the Spessart Hills had formerly been private royal hunting grounds that over the course of time were transferred to the archbishops and electors of Mainz. Naturally, these men of God had a commercial interest in preserving and caring for their fine old oak and beech trees and due to this fact, the Spessart Hills remains one of the largest continual forested areas in the country. Nowadays, upward mobility means a commute to one of the metropolitan areas and the region is no longer home to the poor. And, having a green zone near one's home has attracted many people to the Spessart.

Mighty Walls Tell Tales

The border between the Spessart Hills and the Rhön Hills is more or less where the Sinn River ▶ turns south. In the high Middle Ages, the lower Sinn valley was the home of the counts of Rieneck who set about taking on the bishops in Mainz and Würzburg by creating their own territory. The extinction of the family line in1559 passed the question of power on to Mainz. Their family seat located above the town of the same name then fell into disrepair. Little remains of their fortress ▲ but art lovers won't want to miss the Romanesque chapel ◀ in the main tower. The tower itself is somewhat of a curiosity since it is seven-sided on the exterior and octagonal in the interior. This highly unusual architectural construction houses an original Romanesque altar.

It was the topography that convinced settlers to settle on the rise near the Main River where there was little danger of flooding. The city walls were built into the surrounding slopes and from the very beginning, Lohr began growing and soon became the logical regional center between the woods and the river ◀. In medieval times a fortress stood where the castle now stands near the church. The forests provided the building material clearly evident along the Hauptstrasse ▼ where patrician half-timbered buildings line the street. The electors of Mainz, on the other hand, built their castle ▶ out of stone.

Imposing Elegance in Lohr

A Countryside Reflecting Bygone Days

The Hafenlohr River ◄ has the width of a stream and it meanders through a valley far too wide to make the river's presence felt. The river takes its time, dillydallying at every bend, enjoying the scenic valley slopes along the 25-kilometer stretch before it empties into the Main River ►. The crystal-clear stream flows past a few hamlets and through uninhabited forests. During a visit in Lichtenau in 1927, the writer, Kurt Tucholsky, described the valley in the following manner: "This is a countryside that no longer exists." Fortunately, for 21st century man, the Hafenlohr valley still does exist and, through the good works of numerous conservationists, it will continue to exist. Plans to build a reservoir would put an end to this meandering stream.

scendents of the Echter-Ingelheim lineage still reside in the castle, which, in itself, is a museum with several rooms open to the public. Each room and every nook and cranny are bursting with the family collections gathered over a several hundred year period. Among the treasures is the baptismal gown of Julius Echter, who later became prince-bishop in Würzburg, as well as militarily-effective body armor ▼.

Fairytale Castle in the Forest

Well-hidden among the trees, the moated castle ▲ that nowadays serves as a romantic tourist attraction is actually the family home of the imperial counts of Ingelheim, better known as the Echter family of Mespelbrunn who formerly served as hereditary administrative officials in Mainz. This small castle dates back to 1419 but its charming appearance in a magnificent setting is due to renovations made in the 19ᵗʰ century ▶. De-

Mainz Held Court in Aschaffenburg

If Johann Schweikard von Kronberg were to be elected archbishop of Mainz, he had to promise in 1604 to build a new castle in Aschaffenburg. Johannisburg Castle was inhabited by 1615, proof that politicians sometimes actually kept their promises ◀ ▲.

Johannisburg Castle, undoubtedly the best example of German Renaissance castle-building ◀, served a representative function well into the 18th century. The only thing it lacked was a large park around it. Ever since Jean Jacques Rousseau had infested all of Europe with his "back to nature" creed, it became de rigueur at court to have an English garden, which was to imitate nature as closely as possible. Park Schönbusch, one of the first gardens of this kind on the European continent, was completed in 1776 for the last archbishop of Mainz. Artistically laid-out paths wind through the park and lead to the occasional folly such as a miniature castle ▶ or the Temple of Friendship ▲.

The German Renaissance and an English Garden in Franconia

based on the genuine villa was typical for the era. The Pompejanum does have a classical atrium ◄◄, in the middle that served as an inner courtyard and source of light. Original Roman sculptures such as that of a black marble dancing satyr ▼ add authenticity to the ambience.

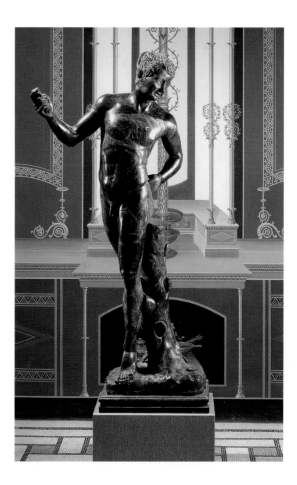

A Satyr Finds a Home in Pompeii on the Main

Although Aschaffenburg enjoys a relatively mild climate, the Classical Roman Pompejanum above the vineyards overlooking the Main River ▲ seems to stretch the imagination just a tad. Between 1840 and 1848, King Ludwig I had a house, destroyed by Vesuvius in AD 79, reconstructed in the same dimensions and called it his "Bavarian Nice." The king wanted to provide his subjects with a visual example of a Pompeian villa and, at the same time, demonstrate his taste for and knowledge of antiquity. The fact that the "House of Castor and Pollux" was only loosely

A Charitable Institution and Alzenau Fortress

The original center of Aschaffenburg was St. Peter and Alexander Collegiate Church ◀. By means of generous contributions, its royal founders, the electors of Mainz, became one of the largest landowners in the Spessart Hills. The significance of this charitable foundation can still be experienced at the square dominated by the church. The well-preserved cloisters are some of the loveliest in all of Germany ▲.

The electors of Mainz also had a fortress built in the last decade of the 14th century in Alzenau ▶. Although it is mainly a ruin, it is considered to be an excellent example of late medieval fortress construction.

In 1506, the German humanist, Johannes Butzbach, described Franconian viticulture as such: "Rows and rows of vineyards cover the slopes; despite this fact, the brain never gets confused and the heart is overjoyed." Mr. Butzbach, a resident of Miltenberg, would most likely feel the same today. And, the steep slopes between Klingenberg ◄ and Bürgstadt in the Main River valley continue to produce quality wines. For decades, the rule of thumb in Franconia was: red sandstone means red wine. This still applies today because the best Franconian red wines do grow in the red sandstone soil of the Spessart Hills and the Odenwald Forest. In the 18th century, the Catholic branch of the counts von Löwenstein had a castle-like residence built along the Main River although their choice of location had little to do with the natural beauty of the area. Their intent was to escape the constant quarrels with their Protestant relatives in Wertheim. They chose Kleinheubach ▼ and contracted the Hessian court architect, Louis Remy de la Fosse. A patrician version of this residence can be found at the foot of Mildenburg Fortress in Miltenberg ►.

Where Red Wine Thrives
in Franconia

In 1368, Miltenberg was awarded the staple right that stipulated that all goods transported on the Main River had to be offered for sale for a few days in the town. Throughout the 16th and 17th centuries the merchants displayed their wealth in the magnificently gabled, half-timbered buildings like the ones that surround the Market Square ◀ and line the Hauptstrasse ▶ or Main Street, which prided itself as the economic hub of the town and the charming Renaissance façade of Hotel Riesen ▼ or Giant demonstrates the wealth of the past.

Half-timbered Splendor in Miltenberg

Glorious Cloisters in Amorbach

Although the name of the town, Amorbach ▼, speaks of love, the name has actually little to do with the feeling itself. According to legend, a certain Amor, a student of the Benedictine missionary, St. Pirmin, built a simple monk's cell on the spot in 730. For some strange reason, his reliquaries had to be brought back from Maastricht in the 15th century. Saints were known to travel, especially after their deaths. After years of turbulence, the Benedictine monastery finally enjoyed its heyday in the 18th century. The medieval buildings were completely renovated, leaving only the two medieval

church towers intact. Maximilian von Welsch, an architect from Mainz, designed the new church  in the jubilant Rococo style so appropriate for the illustration of heavenly glory. The Wildenburg ruins ▲▶ , however, speak of a far different splendor. The structure is reminiscent of many an imperial palace of the period and pays tribute to the renowned 12th century architect, Ruprecht von Dürn, one of the Staufer emperors foremost and closest confidants. The peasants set fire to the noble structure during the Peasants' War in 1525.

Wertheim, situated at the point where the Tauber flows into the Main, used to be considered the Franconian version of the city of Koblenz on the Rhine. There is no good reason for such a striking town to play second fiddle to the likes of Koblenz. The attractive location on two rivers ▶ under the protection of a fortress on a rocky cliff ▼ ensured its economic growth. The fact that the town floods on a regular basis is of lesser importance. The quaint Old Town continues to thrive despite the water. Stadtprozelten had and has just as little space to spread out. It is squeezed in between the river and the outcrop of a hill, home of the mighty Henneburg ruins ◀.

Ruins Stand Guard on the Main River

It is true that the entire current structure of St. Jacob's Church in Urphar isn't a thousand years old; yet, the beginnings of this small church certainly date back to the 10th century. Whether it be the decorative metal fittings on the door ▼ or the simple sanctuary inside ▶, the entire church emits a feeling of a safe, heavenly haven. Both the church and the village owe their existence to a ford in the Main River that makes a loop ◀ around this so-called heavenly place.

Thousand-year-old Church in a Heavenly Place

Red Cliffs and Trickling Rocks

Rothenfels or Red Cliff is one of few fortresses ◄ that have been preserved along the Main River. Its shimmering red sandstone façade lends a forceful addition to the village below bearing the same name. This picturesque hamlet, situated between the narrow strip of land below the red cliffs and the river, is the smallest in Bavaria. Triefenstein Monastery ▲, named after the numerous springs that trickle down the rocks, is a few kilometers further down the Main River.

A Triangle Full of Grapes

A Geometric Design on the Main

The numerous turns and bends that the Main River takes have often led to imaginative interpretations. Many an observer has commented on all the things that can be read into studying a map of the Main valley. The Main River Triangle and the Main River Square are the easiest to pick out and the Main River Square is easy to give a name to since it encompasses the Spessart Hills. It becomes a bit more difficult with the Main River Triangle because upon closer inspection, there are actually two. No one ever speaks of the one whose points are Urphar-Gemünden-Würzburg. The Main

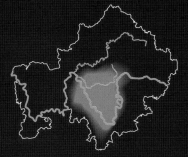

◀ *The hills can be gently rolling or steep near Himmelstadt*

River Triangle everyone is familiar with is the Triangle encompassing the area surrounding Gemünden-Ochsenfurt-Schweinfurt. The first triangle is smaller and more rural and is hardly ever thought of as a triangle. The two triangles together make up the hub of Franconian viniculture with the largest portion of grapes being grown in the larger Main River Triangle. Viticulture in Franconia was first documented in 777 in Hammelburg, a town that has more in common with the Rhön Hills than winegrowing. Hammelburg belonged to the monastery in Fulda so it was natural that wine would be grown on its slopes. The monks not only needed the wine to celebrate communion; they also used wine as a source of income to finance their extensive building projects. As early as the 8th century, monasteries in Holzkirchen, Ochsenfurt, Kitzingen and Schwarzach played a significant role in both developing the countryside and growing wine. Wine was considered the hard currency of the entire region; sometimes it served as the sole currency. At the end of the 18th century, Franconia was number one in wine export in the Holy Roman Empire of the German Nation. Wine was grown on approximately 16,000 hectares whereas in the Middle Ages, up to 40,000 hectares were planted in grapes in Franconia. Everyone profited from viniculture: the winegrowers themselves, farmers, burghers, merchants, barrel-makers, civil servants and, of course, the nobility. Wine

made money; money made the building of representative town halls, fortified city walls, stately churches and innumerable patrician homes possible. Tilman Riemenschneider's woodcarvings and altars could not have been realized without the wealthy wine patrons in Main-Franconia. His magnificent Madonna in the Rose Garland in the midst of Volkach's gentle vine-covered slopes seems to have been carved in gratitude for the surrounding vineyards. Wine did not, however, enjoy a fixed interest rate. Weather conditions were scrutinized year in, year out, until the last grapes were off the vine. Poor yields were more common in the past than nowadays. In 1786, for example, a bill from the charitable institution in Iphofen read: "Three consecutive years of extremely poor harvests means that even with the use of military force, taxes cannot be collected." The weather report and the economic report were one and the same and during poor harvest years, large projects such as the completion of the Residence in Würzburg could be brought to a halt not to mention the numerous wars that were fought on a regular basis. During the Thirty Years' War, the vineyards in Main-Franconia were abandoned for so many years that in 1643, the Hofbräu brewery could be established in Würzburg, the stronghold of wine, despite the cries of

▲ *The castle in Rimpar owes its ornate design to the bishops in Würzburg*

outrage from the winegrowers. Viticulture nevertheless survived and Catholic winegrowers could normally depend upon St. Urban, their patron saint and "link to heaven." In the fields surrounding the Catholic villages, it is hard to miss the many wayside shrines that give testimony to requests for a plentiful harvest. Protestant winegrowers had no other option than to turn directly to God, which saved them from having to spend money to erect wayside shrines. Winegrowers of both faiths had to deal with poor harvests and in order to survive, they had to calculate the good years keenly and save for the bad years. No amount of faith could prevent the harm done by the hungry phylloxera in the 19th century. These lice literarily gnawed on the roots of prosperity and destroyed one vineyard after the other. The phylloxera had been a stowaway on a ship from America carrying grapevines in its hull. Franconian wines were nearing extinction until the middle of the 20th century when a combination of grafting an American root to a European vine above the surface proved successful. Viniculture began to thrive again and larger areas were set aside for vineyards. At the end of World War II there were around 2,400 hectares of wine growing in Franconia; nowadays wine grows on around 6,000 hectares. Wine towns too, have taken a turn for the better. They have become the architectural highlights of the region and their charm adds to the ambiance of the countryside.

▼ *Homburg ruin is one of the largest fortress ruins in southern Germany*

Holzkirchen Monastery was founded in 775 and for over a thousand years this religious center's monks served the needs of this remote rural region. As a subsidiary of the affluent abbey in Fulda, the monastery also played a significant economic role thanks to its widespread holdings. As late as the 18th century, things were going so well that none other than the court architect, Balthasar Neumann, was commissioned to build a new church ◀ in Holzkirchen. His French inspired dome is a pleasant contrast to the other Franconian half-timbered buildings in the complex.

Homburg on the river Main is close by and it too played an important religious role in the history of Main-Franconia. It is said that the first bishop of Würzburg died in a grotto beneath the half-timbered castle ▶▶ that was later built. The rocky cliff above the river was a good strategic point for a fortress and topographic limitations prevented this influential town from spreading. The townspeople of the nearby town of Marktheidenfeld outmatched Homburg by building a bridge across the river in the 19th century. Now as in the past, Homburg is most renowned for its superb wines. This fact didn't keep the townspeople from looking for a less volatile form of income as the restored paper mill built in 1807 proves. ▶

An 8th Century House of Worship in Holzkirchen

A bird's eye view of Karlstadt reveals a carefully laid-out medieval town with block after block of right-angled streets and buildings. The city planners in 1200 did, however, build the structures on a slight curve to reveal more of the architectural nuances of the facades ◀. The Karlsburg ruin ▶, destroyed by the burghers in 1525, comes into full view in the Maingasse ▼.

Karlsburg Fortress Keeps Watch Over a Medieval Town

Thüngen Castle  has been in the same baronial family since its very beginnings some 800 years ago. A closer look behind the castle walls reveals architectural elements from nearly every epoch. Medieval construction was less evident after the peasants released their rage on the feudal lords in 1525. New construction was carried out and later, in keeping with the times, Baroque and neo-Gothic additions were incorporated. It was Konrad von Thüngen who as prince-bishop in Würzburg defeated the peasants in Franconia. It was this same member of the Thüngen line that kept Tilman Riemenschneider locked up for nearly two months in the Marienberg Fortress where he was mercilessly interrogated. Shortly before the Peasants' War, Riemenschneider had completed the Mourning of Christ ▶, a deeply religious and moving relief that now hangs in the village church of Maidbronn. Riemenschneider depicted himself in the figure of Nicodemus holding a saltbox at the foot of the Cross. It is said to have been Riemenschneider's last portrait before the Peasants' War, the Reformation and the beginning of the Renaissance that brought his rapid career to a tragic halt.

A Prince-Bishop from Thüngen
Confronted the Peasants

The prince-bishops used their modest palace in Veitshöchheim as a hunting lodge until it was enlarged and refined in the 18th century when it became the ideal summer retreat ◄ from the heat and humidity in Würzburg. In the 1760s, Prince-bishop Adam Friedrich von Seinsheim had the grounds turned into a Rococo pleasure park enhanced by playful follies, a Chinese pavilion ► and innumerable elegant statures such as the group representing spring ▼.

The Bishop's Summer Retreat

Veitshöchheim's Geometric Garden

The artistic geometric design of the court gardens ▶ in Veitshöchheim is a joy to walk through. The main pond features the large sculpture of Mt. Parnassus whose muses represent a new world order. Nearby, an antique ruin ▲ next to a cascade is reminiscent of the old world order.

Wine, Wealth and Music

Wine has been growing on the sun-soaked slopes of the Teufelskeller and the Sonnenstuhl ◀ in Randersacker since 779. As in most hamlets in Main-Franconia, stately inner courtyards throughout the village make it evident that viticulture was and is a profitable undertaking. Vintage wines also made it possible for the neighboring village of Eibelstadt to erect such a lovely town hall and parish church at the Market Square ▲.

Trade and Transition Characterize Marktbreit and Ochsenfurt

It may not be evident at first glance, but until the railroad began passing through in the 19th century, Marktbreit was a major port. Trade consisted of unloading the boats and transporting the goods overland: a lucrative business reflected in numerous fine merchants' houses ▲. The banks of the Breitbach stream were extremely narrow but romantically picturesque: the "Painter's Corner" ▶ at the Main Gate is a good example. A few kilometers downstream, half-timbered buildings ◀ also flank the old streets in Ochsenfurt. This fortified town was once the center of exchange for products from the fertile, outlying farmsteads.

83

An Old Cellar and Impious Nuns

Kitzingen owed its affluence to wine, the river, and the stone bridge over the river. Pleasant 16th to 18th century patrician houses at the Market Place ◀ bear witness to this fact. It all began in a Benedictine Nunnery; only the 8th century cellar has survived. The nunnery itself was dissolved around 500 years ago; discipline with its walls was reputed to be very lax. The town, on the other hand, flourished nicely and enjoyed the luxury of two confessions. Two stately churches as well as the towers of the synagogue dominate the skyline now ▶ as in the past. The Baroque façade of St. Ursula's ▲ is noteworthy as well.

Vogelsburg ▶, a former convent, and Volkach ▶▶. There is no river traffic along this stretch but wayside shrines like the moving Gray Torture from 1511 accompany the traveler ▼.

Thick Walls in a Scenic Countryside

The number of watchtowers, over 50 in total, which once protected Dettelbach ▲ had to have set a record. Their military significance was minimal but their symbolic significance was what counted: the city had received a city charter in 1484. Aside from the watchtowers, the surrounding countryside gives no indication of being anything but gentle especially at the wide, shallow bend in the Main River Loop between

Grapevines and a Rose Garland

Volkach's Market Place ▶ boasts a proud Renaissance Town Hall, the perfect backdrop for tasting the prestigious Volkacher Ratsherr wines. The Ratsherr or councilman is symbolic of grapes grown on the slopes of the same name that surround Mary in the Vineyards Pilgrimage Church ▲. Although plain on the outside, the sanctuary inside attracts worshippers of the Virgin Mary and art connoisseurs alike. Tilman Riemenschneider carved Mary in the Rose Garland ◀, a mature late work, in 1524.

Schweinfurt's number one export item, the ball bearing, has ensured that things run smoothly worldwide. Friedrich Fischer's invention in 1850 turned a former free imperial city into one of Franconia's major industrial cities. This industrious industrial city does, however, boast several buildings worthy of note such as the palatial Renaissance Town Hall at the Market Square ◀ and St. Johannis Lutheran Church ▼. Not a trace of industry is evident in Werneck, a few kilometers south of Schweinfurt, where in the 18th century the prince-bishops of Würzburg had a summer palace built ▶ that was nearly as grand as their Residence in Würzburg.

Ball Bearings and a Summer Palace:
Schweinfurt and Werneck

History Characterizes the Present

Würzburg – Main-Franconia's Cultural Center

"A magnificently beautiful city" are the words Wolfgang Amadeus Mozart used to describe his succinct but unequivocal opinion of Würzburg during his brief stopover in 1790 on his way to the coronation of Leopold II as Holy Roman Emperor in Frankfurt. Perhaps Mozart was speculating on a court appointment. Little did he realize that the enlightened Prince-bishop Franz Ludwig had no real appreciation for music and the arts. Thus Würzburg's chance of becoming a city of Mozart was dashed before it began. Nonetheless, since 1921, an annual Mozart Festival has been held in the Resi-

◀ *Würzburg: the four towers of the Romanesque Cathedral*

dence. Mozart was by no means the only one who held such a high opinion of the prince-bishop's city on the Main River. Goethe, as well, is said to have considered Würzburg one of the loveliest cities in Germany. His favorable words may have been somewhat influenced by the locally-grown Stein wine. In a letter written in 1801, Goethe revealed that after having tasted Stein wine, no other would suffice. Even the later author of Steppenwolf, Hermann Hesse, a man who made no bones about what he thought of Catholicism, confessed, "If I were a budding poet and wanted to choose my place of birth, I would certainly give Würzburg careful consideration. This lovely city leaves me with the impression that it has something to offer a born poet." These are hymns of praise spanning three hundred years for a city that in reality no longer exists. Bomb attacks over Würzburg on March 16, 1945, destroyed this splendid city on the Main River and turned it into a red-hot "grave on the Main." A city that had been flourishing for centuries ceased to exist; a portion of Old Europe vanished forever. What would men like Mozart, Goethe or Hesse think of Würzburg nowadays? Could Mozart, in view of the high-rise apartment complex on the hill and industrial zoning still enjoy a coffee break here? Can Stein wine muddle the mind enough to still find the city enchanting? Hermann Hesse would have to correct himself and

admit that this city, despite its numerous cultural sights, boasts one chain store after the other and uninspiring postwar architecture in the downtown area. It no longer stands out as a place where writers come to be inspired. Fortunately, Würzburg has survived and despite many poor architectural decisions that were made during the postwar years and despite all the changes that have turned a once traditional bishopric into a modern center for the services industry, Würzburg has managed to preserve its original unique character. It remains a city, unlike most other large German cities, that presents itself as the summation of its past. It helps to become acquainted with the history of Würzburg because the city's past is useful in understanding the historical monuments that have been rebuilt to their past glory. For 1300 years, Christianity has been the driving force, the determining factor in the city's history. It began with three Irish missionaries, Kilian, Todnan and Kolonat who introduced the Christian faith to Main-Franconia in the last quarter of the 7th century. It has been argued that Christianity played a major role in every old European city and that Würzburg was not unique; instead, it was one of many. This

▲ *The Stift Haug Church and the Cathedral soar above the rooftops; the Käppele Chapel is on the hill*

argument fails to hold water since the city was a home to Christianity whose administrators were clergymen. Ever since the founding of the bishopric, Christianity has also been the most important worldly power. A secular aristocratic family of regional Frankish-Thuringian dukes died out so quickly that no traces remain. When Boniface founded the bishopric in 741 or 742 in order to get a better grip on Christian souls, the first bishop, Burkhart, who would later be canonized, had no worldly competition in this small settlement and he automatically became the town sovereign. Later, he received the title of prince and beginning with the Staufer dynasty, the bishop bore the prestigious title of duke in Franconia. From the very start, secular Würzburg burghers and religious Würzburg burghers had an almost symbiotic relationship. As often as the townspeople of the high and late Middle Ages clashed with the secular power of the church and as much as they sought to quarrel with the bishops they despised, even the most irreconcilable townsfolk had to admit that without their bishops, Würzburg would never have enjoyed any supraregional significance. In the 18th century, these very same prince-bishops had a palace built, one that remains the high point of a visit to this city. What would Würzburg be without

▶ *Wine connoisseurs have been on a pilgrimage to Stachel Wine Inn for almost 600 years*

"its" world famous Residence, a superb monument to political insignificance? Would it be a larger version of the neighboring town of Ochsenfurt? It is a waste of time to speculate the issue. Würzburg has come to accept the diverse dual powers of its former prince-bishops, their Residence in the city and the Marienberg Fortress on the hill. The city sees itself as a vital part of the 21st century... and as "a magnificent, beautiful city."

The Old Main Bridge – Belvedere and Eye-catcher

The best economic investment the city made in the entire Middle Ages was the erection of the Old Main Bridge ▲ over 850 years ago. The elegant arches were a part of later renovations; it wasn't until the Baroque that the larger-than-life statues of saints, the triumphal axis of religious beliefs, gave the bridge its true meaning: this Via Triumphalis leads from the fortress to the Cathedral ◄. In fact, a bridge gate was torn down to improve the view of the Cathedral!

Marienberg Fortress – Fortified Proof of the Bishop's Power

Previous generations may have respected the fact that Marienberg Fortress ▶ was Würzburg's landmark, but they were hardly fond of the idea. The fortifications brought to mind the unpopular reign of the prince-bishops during the Middle Ages. The bishop was far too well aware that if his authority were to survive, it needed to be walled in. More than once the townspeople attempted an attack in order to rid themselves of their sovereign. Around 1200, a castle and fortifications were begun with a dual purpose of protecting the bishop while providing him with a magnificent residence worthy of his power. Its location high above the town kept this symbol of the bishop's sovereignty ever-present, especially in conjunction with the Old Main Bridge ◀ or the Old Crane ▲.

Defeat and its Consequences or How the Swedes Revived the Construction Industry

A bird's eye view of Marienberg Fortress reveals just how large this complex really is. Powerful walls surround the living quarters and outbuildings. Advanced triangular bastions made it possible to take the attacker under fire from multiple directions. Particularly remarkable is the concentration of bastions on the west side ◄. This was the Achilles' heel of the Marienberg and the Swedes used this avenue of approach to storm the fortress in 1631. In consequence, after the Treaty of Westphalia, there was an enormous reinforcement with bastions and new gates such as the Neutor or New Gate ▲. The inner courtyard did retain its castle keep, well house and 7th century Mary's Church ► after which the fortress was named.

The Treasure Trove of Main-Franconian Art

Marienberg Fortress ▶, which had been expanding for hundreds of years, was turned to rubble on March 16, 1945. Incendiary bombs were dropped on the city and the fortress where major damage was done. The fortress was rebuilt and now houses convention halls, the Bavarian state archives, two restaurants and two museums. The Main-Franconian Museum is undoubtedly the main attraction with its impressive collection of artworks and Franconian culture on display in the former arsenal and Echter bastion. The museum is the successor to the bombed out Franconian Luitpold Museum whose art treasures, in large part, could be brought to safety in time. Now as in the past, the late Gothic works of Tilman Riemenschneider, especially his Adam and Eve ◀, are the highlights of the museum.

Fanciful Delicacy Greets the Fortress

When Balthasar Neumann was commissioned to build a new chapel next to the 17th century Virgin of Mercy Chapel, he knew that his architecture would have to compete with the immense fortifications one hill over ◀. Thus the front of the Baroque chapel or Käppele faces the town ▽▶ and the undulating lines of its delicate façade and sweeping spires make it appear like a ballerina dancing next to a weightlifter. Very few locals are aware of the fact that the Käppele's real name is "The Visitation."

From the Käppele or the Marienberg, the number of church towers rising above the rooftops seems enormous. For centuries, the spires of faith of Mary's Chapel, Neumünster Church, University Church and the Cathedral ◄▼ have been dominating the city's silhouette attesting to the prominent role the church has always played. The Town Hall tower is the only secular representative in the ensemble. In the midst of these proud towers stands the church with the longest tradition: modest St. Burkard's ▶. Formerly a knightly charitable institution, it does boast a splendid Gothic choir.

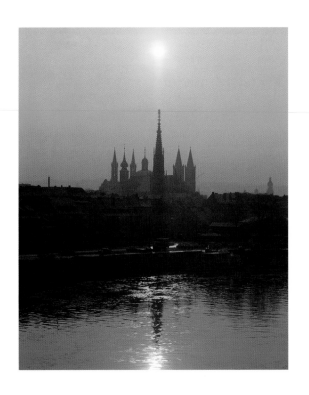

A Skyline of Faith:
Würzburg's Church Towers

"We Praise You, We Thank You

…Your children in Franconia, St. Kilian." This is the text that is sung the first Sunday in July during a procession that goes from Neumünster Church to the Cathedral next door bearing the reliquaries of the Franconian apostle, Kilian. An imposing octagonal Baroque dome marks the place where over 1300 years ago, Kilian, Kolonat and Todnan met a martyr's death on behalf of their religious beliefs. The stunning façade of Neumünster Church ◀ is a masterpiece of theatricality; it is a demonstration of the alliance between pathos and sensitivity. The Romanesque arcades ▼ in the former cloister behind the church offer a quiet, meditative contrast.

The Cathedral – a Living Monument and Museum

While the Cathedral was being built in the 11th century, everyone was sure that none of the builders and clerics would live to see its completion. This huge project constructed to the glory of God united several generations of families and various social classes. The exterior of the Cathedral ▲, the fourth largest Romanesque Cathedral in German-speaking countries, emits an austere medieval view of religion. The interior contains ▶ works of art spanning the epochs of time. The heart of the bishopric has become a museum of the pious.

111

The Burghers and a Count's Death

In 1316 the burghers of Würzburg helped Knight Kuno vom Rebstock get out of an embarrassing debt by buying the stone building that later became known as the "Green Tree." Over the years, the city council enlarged the 12th century structure and turned it into an impressive symbol ▶ of civic self-assuredness. The highlight of the Town Hall is the late Romanesque Wenceslas Hall ◀, which dates back to the 13th century and was named after the 14th century German King Wenceslas. The city fathers had hoped that the king would make Würzburg a free imperial city but this unpredictable heavy drinker and weak ruler was the wrong man to rely on; the city's dream of independence was extinguished in 1400 when Würzburg troops were defeated at the Battle of Bergtheim. The tower was raised to its current height in the 15th century to serve as a fire depot and to compete more effectively with the surrounding church spires. The Town Hall, an architectural potpourri of styles, also goes by the name of Grafeneckart. The name is derived from a 12th century mayor, Graf or Count Eckart, who was murdered in front of the building.

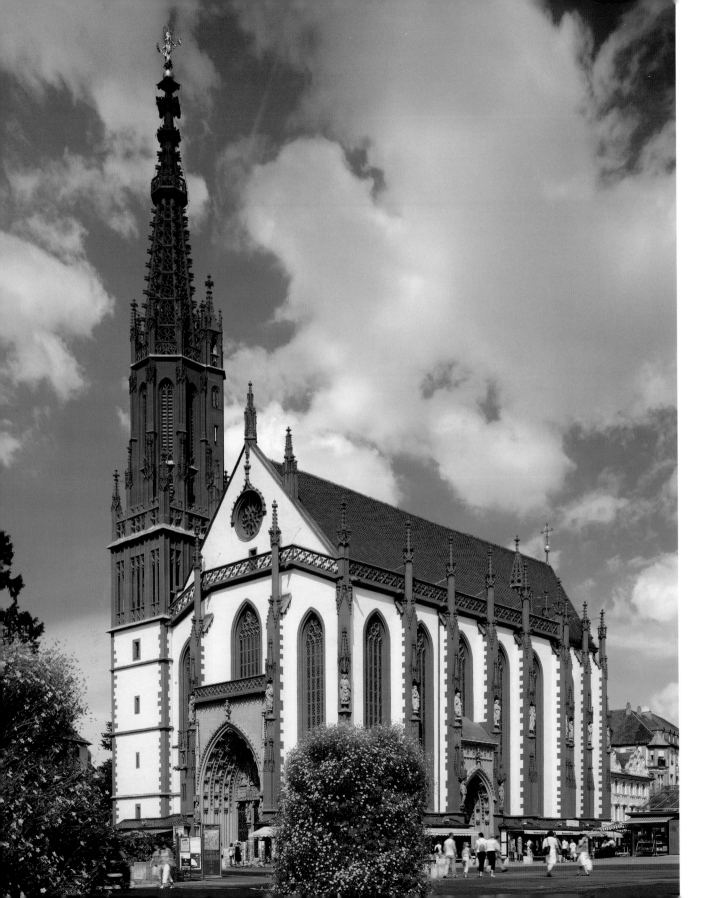

The Secular Meets the Spiritual

Mary's Chapel and the House to the Falcon ▶ stand side by side at the upper Market Place. Both compete architecturally but offer the observer quite a contrast. The 14th/15th Gothic church is decorated with transparent filigree spires ◀ reaching towards the heavens while the playful stuccowork of the 18th century House to the Falcon ▼, formerly an inn, emphasizes horizontal lines that are securely anchored in this world. The Rococo satisfied one's earthy needs while the Gothic took care of one's spiritual needs – a brilliant appropriation on the Market Place.

In 1576 Prince-bishop Julius Echter von Mespelbrunn had a charitable institution built for those who could no longer help themselves as a visible sign of benevolence. Renowned as the first example of a modern large-scale institution, new construction in the 17th century turned the garden wing ◄ into an outstanding Baroque palace where the bishop resided when he was in town. Even the apothecary ▲ was ornately decorated in the 18th century, turning a purely functional room into an appealing work of art.

The Juliusspital:
Do Good and Spread the Word

Artworks instead of Grain at the Old Harbor

The Granary or Kulturspeicher ▲ at the Old Harbor has been functioning as an art gallery since 2001. The sweeping gables of the exterior emit an air of "commercial art deco" while the interior features works from the past 200 years including a superb collection of conceptual art. This ambitious project to present modern art in a city known for Riemenschneider and Neumann has become a tremendous success. The wooden beams in the foyer ◄ are reminiscent of the building's original function.

Europe's Loveliest Parsonage

...is what Napoleon is said to have called the Residence in Würzburg. More likely, his subtle sarcasm referred to the extraordinary size of an abode for a clergyman, but it can also be interpreted literally to mean the "palace of palaces," the most lavish and architecturally significant castle ever constructed for a prince-bishop. The 170-meter garden façade alone ▶ would have easily satisfied most kings and emperors. Built in conjunction with the plans of several architects, it was Balthasar Neumann who was commissioned to oversee construction between 1720 and 1744. The Residence was more than a place for the prince-bishop to live: it was the manifestation of Würzburg as a bishopric as well as the manifestation of the claims of the ambitious Schönborn family. Strangely enough, neither the bishopric nor the Schönborn family was truly a part of Europe's elite. In light of this fact, the description of the Residence by the art historian, Georg Dehio, seems appropriate. He called the Residence an "historical pipedream."

Tiepolo's World Theater Gives an Enjoyable Performance

No matter how many high-ranking, illustrious guests glided up the Grand Staircase in the Residence, it was always Balthasar Neumann's breathtaking interior design ◀◀ and Giambattista Tiepolo's phenomenal fresco ceiling of the four known continents that stole the show. It was the prince-bishop who bathed in the glory of receiving his guests in such oversized stately rooms. The sumptuous ambiance made it clear what the owner thought of both himself and his guests. Asia, Africa, America ◀ and Europe ▲ are depicted as female figures gathered around to pay tribute to the bishop in Würzburg. High above all the earthly hustle and bustle, the sovereign patron, Prince-bishop Karl Philipp von Greiffenclau, sits grandly in a medallion ▲ surveying the world below.

121

The Consequences of a Coffee Break

When Wolfgang Amadeus Mozart made a stopover in Würzburg on his way to Frankfurt, he barely had enough time for a cup of coffee and the observation that Würzburg was a magnificently beautiful city. He never would have dreamed that 130 years later, this very city would begin sponsoring a Mozart Festival dedicated solely to his musical genius. Each year the Mozart Festival attracts music lovers to the Imperial Hall in the Residence ◀ where an internal marriage of architecture, statues and paintings are brought to life through Mozart's congenial music. Neumann, Tiepolo and Bossi form the "artistic triumvirate" that created the most well balanced Rococo interior of illusions: a feast for all the senses. This illusion extends beyond the thick walls as becomes evident in the Court Gardens between the Residence and the old city walls. The garden façade of the palace is the ideal backdrop for an outdoor performance of Mozart's ▶ "Eine kleine Nachtmusik."

The Residence Apartments: an Exquisite Blend of Rococo and Classicism

Prince-bishop Friedrich Karl von Schönborn himself came up with the bizarre idea of a Cabinet of Mirrors ◄◄ to show off his artwork. In order for the room to appear infinite, glass or painted mirrors covered the walls to fool the eye of the observer who lost himself in the illusionary world of reflections and Rococo paintings. Not quite as spectacular, but certainly decorative art of a higher quality can be found in the Green Lacquered Room ▲ with inlay floors that are optical illusions and in the Ingelheim Room ◄.

Vaulted Ceilings for Wine and Incense

The Court Church ◀ remains unparalleled in splendor and what could better befit a prince-bishop? Balthasar Neumann created a room within a room, based on the dynamics of Baroque optical illusions. There are no straight walls; everything seems to be in motion. Light enters through invisible windows and directs a theatrical performance, above which, a vault of bold clouds sways. Gilded altars and marble statues add yet another dimension. Beneath all this sumptuousness, and, once again, beneath a vaulted ceiling, the wine kegs of the Hofkellerei or the State Court Cellars are stored ▶. These formerly belonged to the prince-bishops whose vineyards were spread throughout the surrounding country-side. Some of the wine was used for communion but, for the most, wine was used to pay the salaries of civil servants. Wine was a form of "second currency" when it wasn't in use as the primary currency.

126

Franconia, the symbolic patron saint of Franconia at the fountain in front of the Residence ◀, keeps good company with three famous artists: Tilman Riemenschneider with the Cathedral at his back ▶, Matthias Grünewald bent over his easel ▼, and Walther von der Vogelweide, seated with his legs crossed, reciting one of his own poems. All three men had close links to Main-Franconia. Unfortunately, Balthasar Neumann is not among them, but then again, the greatest monument to Neumann's genius forms the elegant backdrop to his colleagues at the fountain.

A Main-Franconian Triad of Artists

129

Knights Ruled the Hills

The Steigerwald Wood and the Hassberg Hills

The Steigerwald Wood and the Hassberg Hills complement each other extremely well. From a geological standpoint, both groups of hills form one continuous chain that the Main River has been separating for around a million years now. During a warmer period in the formation of our planet, the Upper Main River between Bamberg and Hassfurt broke through the keuper sandstone and began flowing westwards to the Rhine River. These two hilly regions are identical twins from an optical point of view: in the west the hills rise steeply from the valley and in the east, gentle slopes merge comfortably into the broad valleys. The

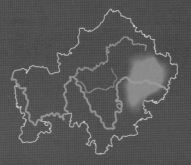

◀ *Vineyards beneath the ruins of the Old Castle in Castell*

131

Steigerwald Wood owes its name to its western portion. The first documented mention of the name dates back to the 12th century when an author was describing the region around Oberschwarzach and Stollberg Hill. From here, the wooded hillside rises steeply and in order to get to the eastern side, the traveler had to climb up a "Steige" or a steep, narrow path. Over time, the term stuck and was used to designate the entire western side of the Steigerwald Wood between Zabelstein and Bullenheim Hill.

Later, when holiday-makers discovered the quiet, scenic beauty of the countryside, the name was extended to the east to the Regnitz River and to the south to the Aisch River.

Although the Steigerwald Wood's name has a descriptive explanation, no origin or meaning of the name has been found to determine why the Hassberg Hills north of the Main River are called such. Some maintain that the word comes from a tribe in Hesse that lived in the region when it was first being settled, but there is no concrete proof. At any rate, this hilly landscape between the sources of the Franconian Saale, the Itz and the Main rivers forms a harmoniously compact area. The region has been able to remain so unspoiled due to the fact that it was virtually off the beaten path, far removed from any major trade roads. Another practical reason may have had something to do with the knightly families who exercised their power here for hundreds of years. Surrounded by the medieval spiritual power centers of Fulda, Würzburg and Bamberg bishoprics as well as the Count von Henneberg, the lesser nobility successfully persevered in standing its ground as was rarely the case anywhere else in Germany. For the most part, the same can be said about the Steigerwald Wood, at least along its western ridge and in the foothills and valleys below. Small wonder that over a third of Lower Franconia's knights and nobility resided in the Hassberg Hills. It is often the case that these castles and fortresses are still inhabited by descendents of the original families. These residences along with the adjacent villages such as Bundorf, Lichtenstein, and Burgpreppach offer a picture-perfect, intact glimpse of days gone by. Although the noble families definitely ruled over their possessions, their role was, by no means, a suppressive one. Unlike elsewhere in central and eastern Germany, aristocratic landowners such as the Rotenhans, Lichtensteins, Truchsesses and Bibras did not take on the typical medieval role of a Junker to maintain their social and political privileges; village inhabitants were not degraded to mere serfdom. Instead, a complex system of old rights and obligations provided for a patriarchal relationship between the aristocracy

▲ *Picturesque ruins are all that remain of Altenstein Fortress*

and its subjects. Moreover, from the very start, landowners were well aware of the fact that the prosperity of their subjects reflected their own prosperity. The more their subjects produced, the higher their feudal obligations. These noble families also depended on their subjects to help them stand firm against the neighboring princes who welcomed any pretext to "selflessly" wield their control over the lesser aristocracy. The majority of the villages in the Hassberg Hills as well as several villages in the Steigerwald Wood have managed to preserve a number of their communal bake houses, breweries and church fortifications. Many of the villages that formerly boasted a rich Jewish community have survived as well. The Jewish cemetery outside of Kleinbardorf is certainly the most impressive; the members of 27 Jewish communities were buried here. There were numerous Jewish communities in this area and the taxes they were obliged to pay were a significant source of income for the landowners.

Hardly a city or town is to be found in the Hassberg Hills or the Steigerwald Wood. On the other hand, noteworthy towns did develop in the foothills and in the outlying valleys. Wine was an important source of income and the proximity of the Main River as a navigation route connected these towns to the outside world. These small agricultural towns present a style all their own and their self-assuredness is evident now as in the past. Iphofen made its fortune from wine, plaster and wood and its well-preserved town walls and three medieval gates bear

▶ *This former administrative castle in Oberschwarzach once belonged to the prince-bishop of Würzburg*

witness to the pride of its inhabitants. Prichsenstadt, the armored dwarf, Zeil, renowned for its half-timbered buildings, and Königsberg with its exotic statue of Roland the Giant are just a few of the gems in a chain of towns among these foothills. Hassfurt and Geroldshofen are city-size in comparison and their landowner, Würzburg's prince-bishop, clearly left his mark. The fortified towns of Eltmann and Ebern don't quite fit into the scheme of things because the one is located in the midst of the Hassberg Hills and the other enjoys the advantage of being situated on the Main River. Both, however, benefited from the auspices of the prince-bishops in Würzburg. All of these isolated towns portray themselves as lovely specimens inconspicuously nestled in a pristine landscape along the eastern border of Lower Franconia.

Wine, Plaster and Wood Make Iphofen Good'

…is written above many an old door in this town at the foot of the Schwanberg Hill ▲. For hundreds of years, these three products guaranteed prosperity to winegrowers, merchants and craftsmen of this charming town that has retained its medieval walls and ditches. Four impressive gates, especially Rödelsee Gate ◀◀, which has earned the reputation of being the quintessential "old Franconian" gate, bears witness to the town's affluence. The massive stone structure appears defiant upon entering the town but protective once inside. The Baroque Town Hall ◀ at the Market Square resembles a miniature palace.

Mönchsondheim: Hammer and Anvil instead of Grain and Wine

The clerestory of Kirchenburg Fortress ◄◄ once served as a granary for the peasants in Mönchsondheim. Everything needed to survive a siege, including wine, was stored here where the attackers had the least chance to plunder. The fortress's construction continued from the 15th to the 18th century. Nowadays, it houses 17 workshops that demonstrate crafts and skills that are becoming extinct such as brush-binding, coopering, blacksmithing and pottery making. These craftsmen bring to life a pre-industrial world that is all too quickly disappearing. Instructors' dormitories in the gatehouse ◄ and the Mesner House ▲ next to the Kirchenburg Gate offer a glimpse of life in a village school.

Walls Turned Peasants into Burghers: Main-Franconia's Small City Culture

Main-Franconia, between the Spessart Hills, Steigerwald Wood and Hassberg Hills, is a region of countless small cities that have enjoyed certain freedoms and privileges since the Middle Ages. There are few such regions in Germany that can boast so many cities with city charters. Würzburg, well-known outside Franconia, as well as Kitzingen and Karlstadt, medium-sized cities that upon closer inspection look more like towns, are more prominent examples. It is really hard to apply the word "city" to hamlets like Prichsenstadt ◄, Rothenfels or Mainbernheim, even when they are protected by watchtowers and fortified gates, contain stately town halls and a number of grand patrician buildings. Actually, these cities lived off the land and their "burghers" were all too familiar with steaming manure heaps, pigsties, winepresses and threshers within their fortified walls. Königsberg at the foothills of the Hassberg Hills was in a league all its own due to its "metropolitan" salt market ►. This Saxon enclave in Franconia was a real city and its inhabitants were more than peasants surrounded by walls.

The Hassberg Hills in Main-Franconia is a cornucopia of fortresses, fortress ruins and storybook castles. At the western foothills, Irmelshausen Castle ◀ built of thick stone walls with half-timbered living quarters is reflected in its own moat. The bizarre ruins ▼ emerging out of the rocky cliff above the Baunach River are all that remain of the original Rotenhan family home. In the 14th century, these imperial barons had a more luxurious castle built near their outbuildings in the valley. The family still resides in Eyrichshof Castle ▶, a fine blend of architectural styles of the 16th to 19th centuries.

Hassberg Hills: Hundreds of Years Old and Still Going Strong

Los Angeles – From Brennhausen and Back

The isolated location of Brennhausen Castle ▼▶ was a better form of protection than its walls. This is one of the very few castles in Lower Franconia that didn't have a village nearby. It remains a beautifully quaint complex that has expanded beyond its two original Gothic watchtowers and living quarters. The castle is accessible during the summer months when its owner, Terry von Bibra, leaves his beech trees behind and heads for the palm trees in LA.

A Parting Word: Aufwiedersehen – Do Return!

No one would dispute that the bends of the Moselle and Saar rivers are truly grand and that the scenic Main River Loop by Volkach ▲ is just as lovely but on a much smaller scale. It is said that great things come in small packages and once the traveler has experienced these rolling hills covered in grape-vines, he will have a hard time forgetting them.